Your Heart and Money:
Uncover the Lies and Live Free

The
Stewardship Movement

Study Guide

Katelyn A. Swiatek

MAP★
FINANCIAL SOLUTIONS

The Stewardship Movement—Study Guide
Published by Tek Inc. (dba MAP Financial Solutions)
4164 Austin Bluffs Pkwy, #122
Colorado Springs, CO 80918

www.MapFinancialSolutions.com

ISBN 978-0-9860910-2-5
ISBN 978-0-9860910-3-2 (electronic)

Published in the United States by Tek Inc. (dba MAP Financial Solutions).

MAP Financial Solutions is a registered trademark of Tek Inc.

Library of Congress Cataloging-in-Publication Data is on file at the Library of Congress, Washington, DC.

Printed in the United States of America

Sales and Author Contact
This book is available at a discount if purchased in bulk. The author is available for training and guest visits. For more information, please email MAP Financial Solutions at info@mapfinancialsolutions.com.

To every believer wondering why money has to be so hard...it doesn't.

In Christ we're made free!

May you find financial freedom during and after this study—

freedom to serve and bless others generously for a lifetime!

Contents

How to Use This Study Guide

Everyone has the ability to be financially free in Christ! The goal of this study is to help you find freedom within your finances so that you can serve and bless others generously.

This study is broken into eight lessons plus conclusion. Each lesson will consist of a video, video guide, follow-up questions, and an exercise section.

- **Video Guide**

  Use this section of your study guide to follow along while you are watching the video for each lesson.

- **Personal Study**

  Use your Personal Study time to explore the topics discussed in the video on a personal level. The personal study consists of follow-up questions and exercises from each video. Be sure to complete each Personal Study before the next video, ensuring that you're prepared to move on to the next lesson.

Money is something we will deal with for the rest of our lives. Why is it that so many of us struggle with it? Why does money have power over us, power that controls our health, mental state, homes, prayer lives, and more? Why did Jesus talk about money so much, and why does the Word talk about money so much? Because how we manage our money affects our relationship with God. What if we're missing something more? What is God calling us to do with the resources we've been blessed with? It's time to understand money for what it really is. Money possesses *no moral bias*. It is simply a medium of exchange. The *moral* structure of money never changes; it is only in the hands of the beholder where money can assume a moral slant. Let's learn how we can manage money in a way that not only glorifies our Father, but also brings others closer to Him. That is what *The Stewardship Movement* is about!

Katelyn

Part I: Learn

Lesson 1—Video Guide

Uncovering the Root

Our Background

- A majority of the time, our views about money originate during

   _____.

Positive Declarations

- Proverbs 18:21

   "The _____ has the power of _____ and _____, and those who

   love it will eat its _____."

- _____ more telling yourself that you're not _____ with numbers!

- Declaring that you're not good with numbers is declaring a _____ over

   your _____.

Money Motives and Attitudes

- The way we manage our money stems from two things:

   1. _____

   2. _____

- In order to start the journey to become financially free, we must start by

   examining our _____ which affect our _____ about

   money.

- Motives originate in the _____.

- Our _____ are revealed in our _____ and _____ of money.

- Money _____ $\longrightarrow$ Money _____ $\longrightarrow$ Money _____

Expecting Perfection

- 1 Samuel 16:7

"But the Lord said to Samuel, 'Do not consider his _____ or his height, for I have _____ him. The Lord does not look at the things man looks at. Man looks at the _____ appearance, but the Lord looks at the _____.'"

- This process isn't about getting it _____ perfect.

- Key Point of Galatians 5:1

It's _____ your _____ standing in the way of your _____ _____. If _____ dictated our _____, then Christ died for _____.

Lesson 1—Personal Study

Uncovering the Root

Uncovering our root motives when it comes to money can be a difficult process that leaves us vulnerable. Even though it's hard, it's necessary before moving forward. The goal is financial freedom, right? Financial freedom in Christ will require a **heart change**. So we start with uncovering the root.

The way we manage money can be linked to two things—motives and attitudes. Correcting your financial management is typically the first step to getting your finances in order. But this can be premature. The first step should be to examine your motives and attitudes about money. In addition to this, you must identify your false beliefs regarding money, which may be holding you back. Therefore, before we learn how to manage a budget, we must first identify what's driving our financial behaviors.

Question One

When you speak, you have the power to speak life or death (Prov. 18:21). This is applicable to anything in our lives, including finances!

Have you ever caught yourself speaking death over your finances? If so, write down the curses you have spoken over your finances and replace them with words of blessing.

<u>**Words of Death (Curse)**</u>   <u>**Words of Life (Blessing)**</u>

1.

2.

3.

Question Two

Take a moment to reflect on three money motives you currently have. Next, write down the attitudes you have developed in order to support these motives. Finally, write down how your money motives and attitudes are reflected in your money management. See the example below.

Example:

In the video, we discussed a gentleman who saved $100,000 by the time he was in his early thirties. His motive was to have savings, and his attitude was, "I will never be without." So he managed his money very conservatively, was very thrifty, and saved diligently.

Motive	*Attitude*	*Money Management*
I want to have savings.	*I will never be without.*	*Conservative*
		Thrifty
		Save diligently

#1)   **Motive**   **Attitude**   **Money Management**

#2)   **Motive**   **Attitude**   **Money Management**

#3)   **Motive**   **Attitude**   **Money Management**

Question Three

Have you ever set a New Year's resolution, only to fail on the first day? When we try to change habits, it can be slow going. This is because habits are so ingrained in who we are, and changing them can be challenging.

When you start to work toward getting your finances in order, you are going to be shifting a lot of habits. Because of this, you need to make sure that you're not holding yourself to a standard of perfection. If you do, you're bound to fail. And failure is discouraging.

Take a moment and list out what you're afraid of in this process:

1.

2.

3.

Question Four

Sometimes our circumstances can feel too big to overcome. You may feel this way about your finances. What did Paul have to say in relation to overcoming trials? Take a moment to read Philippians 4 and write out Philippians 4:13 below.

Exercise

It's time to take the Money Quiz. This quiz is a fun reflection exercise that can help you uncover where your money motives and attitudes may have originated.

Before you take the quiz, make sure you pray. There are going to be questions you may feel are unimportant or too detailed. Give them your best effort. Over the years, I have seen that the effort an individual puts into this quiz directly translates into the effort he or she is willing to put into his or her finances.

This quiz is designed to bring awareness. There are no right answers; there is no score. It's just a mirror for you to see what has been going on in your heart (motives and attitudes) regarding money.

To take the quiz, go to the link below. Print it out and complete the quiz. Then, compare what you answered on the quiz to see if any of the items correlate with Question Two of this Personal Study. If you're married, encourage your spouse to take the quiz, too!

Take The Money Quiz at:
www.TheStewardshipMovement.com

Understanding Poverty and Wealth

Poverty

Poverty Definitions

- Some definitions of the word *poverty* in Scripture are[1]

  _____ _____ _____

  _____ _____ _____

The Poverty Trap

- The United Nations refers to a generational, perpetual cycle of poverty as

  the _____ _____.[2]

- God calls us to bring _____ to the poor by doing three things:

  _____ (Matt. 6:1–4, 25:34–40, Luke 14:12–14)

  _____ (1 John 3:16–18, 2 Cor. 9:6–15)

  _____ (Psalm 113:7–8)

Empathize

- In order to empathize with the poor, we must first understand what

  _____ the poor have to _____.

- Jesus _____ us to become _____ participants in

  the lives of the poor.

- To share and give to the poor, we must first _____ with them.

Share and Give

- Sharing with the poor from one's _____ was a commandment under the Mosaic Law. It is also a commission under the _____ _____.

- Sharing is spurred on by _____.

- Generosity is spurred on by the _____ and at times may seem to defy _____.

Raise Up

- We can raise up the poor by doing three things:

  _____ (1 John 3:16–18)

  _____ (Psalm 82:3–4, Isaiah 1:16–17)

  _____ (Prov. 14:20)

Wealth

Wealth Definition

- Wealth is an _____ of a _____.

- While all of us don't necessarily aspire to be _____, most of us do desire a sense of financial _____ and _____.

- Wealth isn't about stockpiling _____ to _____. It's about sharing our _____ in _____.

Cultivating Wealth

- While all of us don't aspire to cultivate vast amounts of wealth, cultivating wealth can be as simple as creating a _____ zone.

- If we do pursue cultivating wealth, we need to remember three important things:

  1.   (Ecc. 5:15)

  2.   (Ecc. 5:10, 13–14)

  3.   (Ecc. 5:15, Psalm 49:10, 12–20)

- One can cultivate wealth some of the following ways:

  1.   (Gen. 26:12–13, Prov. 10:22)

  2.   (Prov. 19:14, Gen. 25:5)

  3.   (Prov. 10:4)

  4.   (Luke 19:1–2, 1 Chron. 29:26–28)

  5.   (Hab. 2:6, Prov. 22:16)

Motives Check

- When we're focused on _____, wealth can become an addition to our lives rather than the central _____ of our lives.

- When we're focused on _____, wealth can still come, but it may never seem to be _____ because it becomes our focus instead of God.

- A motive that can reflect a focus on self is _____. This can lead to _____, which always leads to a _____ _____.

- A motive that can reflect a focus on God is _____. This can lead to _____, which will lead to _____ _____.

Management of Wealth

- Randy Alcorn states that "our handling of _____ is a litmus test of our true _____."[3]

- The management of our wealth is a culmination of our _____ and _____ coming together.

- If wealth is managed _____, then it can have an eternal impact on the Kingdom.

Lesson 2—Personal Study

Understanding Poverty and Wealth

Since money is a broad subject, I've broken it down into three areas—poverty, wealth, and giving. In this lesson, we will talk about poverty and wealth.

In order to have a better relationship with money and manage it well, we have to understand what God's Word says about poverty and wealth. Some of us may be standing outside of God's will for our lives because we have misconceptions about these topics. Perhaps we've labeled them according to what the world says or what we've been taught. When we explore God's Word on these topics, His heart on them becomes clear. This can open us to move in His will, free from fear or lies that may have been holding us back financially.

Question One

When you hear the word *poverty*, what mental images or words come to mind?

Question Two

In the video, we discussed some scriptural definitions of poverty. From these definitions, has your perception of poverty changed?

Have you ever felt poor? If so, after hearing these definitions, do you still feel poor?

Question Three

God calls us to bring justice to the poor by doing three things: empathizing with them, sharing and giving resources to them, and raising them up.

Let's start with empathy. When we empathize with others, we work to *feel* what they're feeling. God can definitely feel what the poor feel. In order to bless and honor the poor the way that God does, we have to stop and reflect on how we can empathize with them and their trials.

Read Matthew 25:34–40. Below, list out the six things that Jesus is calling us to do for those in need:

Question Four

Sharing and giving to the poor out of one's abundance was a commandment under the Mosaic Law (Exod. 23:10–11). Today, under the New Covenant, we are further commissioned to share and to give to those in need (1 John 3:16–18).

Read 1 John 3:16–24. What question is posed in verse 17? Write it below and then write the answer to the question below the question (verse 18).

Question Five

Raising up the poor is another way we can partner with God to bring them justice. If we can't empathize with them and don't share or give to them, we certainly can't raise them up. Raising up the poor involves acknowledgment, protection, and friendship. Not all of us are called to serve the poor overseas, but there is something we can do from where we are. Take a moment and pray about ministries in your church, city, or around the world that faithfully meet the needs of the poor. I encourage you to take a step in faith and make a commitment to give to one of those ministries so that you might be able to raise up the poor from afar. If you're married and your spouse is not in agreement, wait and pray. God's timing is always perfect.

Write down the ministries that came to mind:

Question Six

Let's transition from the topic of poverty to wealth. Take a moment and reflect on the word *wealth*. What mental images or words come to mind?

Question Seven

Often the word *wealth* gets labeled as ungodly in the Christian community. Review the words you wrote down for Question Six. Would you say a majority of them were negative or positive? Why do you think this is?

Question Eight

It is important to remember that money has no moral bias; it is in the hands of the beholder that this can change. God has blessed many great leaders in biblical history and today with wealth. If you could have a greater sense of financial security and comfort with an increase in finances, would you want it? Do you think it's wrong to desire more? Why or why not?

Question Nine

While I don't believe that it's wrong to desire financial comfort, it's important that we remember three important points: first, hold wealth loosely (it all belongs to God); second, keep your focus on God and not money; and third, always remember that wealth is fleeting. Take a moment and write down what each of these points mean to you.

Question Ten

Until we get our hearts right on the three points we just discussed in Question Nine, pursuing a greater abundance can be dangerous. It is dangerous because, first, if we're too attached to the money, which is fleeting, we could self-destruct if a financial catastrophe were to strike. Second, if we're too focused on money and not on God, we can easily lose our way and get caught up in sins like pride, greed, lust, and more. In the video, we discussed five ways one can cultivate wealth. Which one spoke to you, and why?

Exercise

Cultivating wealth and building it up for current and future provision is not a sin. It is when our focus gets off track that it can become sin. Picture this process like walking a tight path. We must continually be checking our motives to ensure that we're not getting outside of God's will and off track.

In this exercise, you are going to examine your motives regarding wealth. First, you will identify a sinful thought that could get you off track and lead you to a dead end. Second, you will identify a generous thought and one that will lead you to eternal impact. Here's an example:

Focused on Self

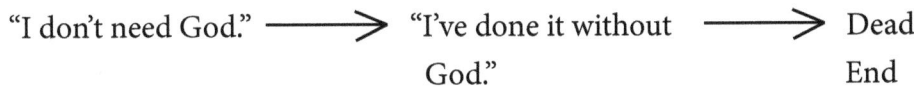

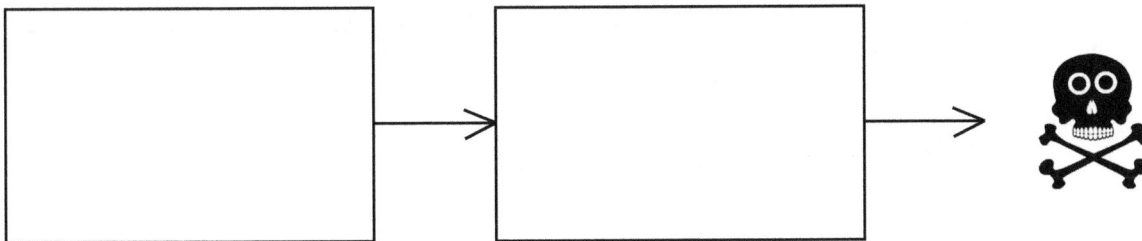

"I don't need God." ⟶ "I've done it without God." ⟶ Dead End

Focused on God

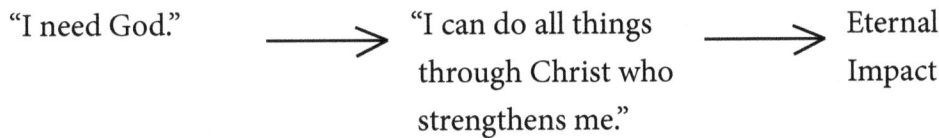

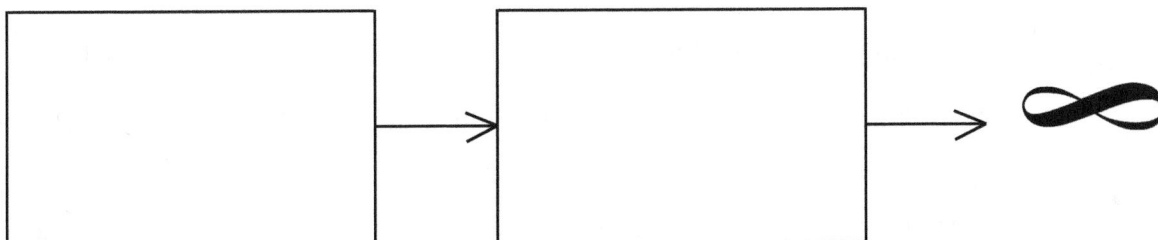

"I need God." ⟶ "I can do all things through Christ who strengthens me." ⟶ Eternal Impact

Focused On Self

Focused On God

The Lack of Nobility in Poverty

Favoritism Forbidden

- God favors neither _____ nor _____.

- In James 2:1–13, church leaders are urged to quit favoring the _____ over the _____.

- In James 2:8–9, James speaks out against _____ _____, _____.

Supernatural Provision

- God can do what may seem _____.

- God _____ just as His Word says He will (_____).

- Money is _____.

Advancing Forward

- Money is a _____ _____.

- Advancing forward isn't about _____ _____; it's about moving _____ and advancing in our _____-given _____.

- When the opportunity is present to be _____ _____ version of us we can

_____ and we're doing _____ about it, we're _____ time.

The Rich Young Ruler and Rich Fool

- The rich young ruler was attached to his _____. (Matt. 19:16–22)

- Jesus reveals to the rich young ruler that he is _____ to _____ with his stuff.

- The parable of the rich fool reveals that _____ is not wrong. It is when we save to _____ _____ in an effort to hoard them for _____. (Luke 12:13–21)

- Jesus is calling us to stop _____ _____ _____ that _____ and to _____ in the _____ instead. (Luke 12:33–34)

- The central theme is this:

Joseph

- Joseph used the _____ from God to save an _____ of _____ for an impending _____.

- When the famine hit, Joseph was able to utilize the _____ stored up to _____ not only himself, but the masses. Joseph stored for _____ provision and also to _____ others. (Gen. 41)

The Lack of Nobility in Poverty

Over the years I have felt that God favored the poor over the wealthy—that if you were wealthy and proclaimed to be a Christian, then perhaps you were missing something. Perhaps you weren't really on track with God.

As a financial counselor, I have experienced many instances in which clients would ask me questions relating to poverty and wealth that I was unable to answer. Matters regarding the types of houses they lived in, the cars they drove, or the amounts they were spending each month—these were all heart matters and were best managed between them and God. Yet there were questions I could answer, those relating to poverty and wealth and what God's Word had to say about each. For too long I felt that poverty was the noble way to live and that wealth would push God out of my life. But when I got into the Word and started to explore these matters, I uncovered that wealth is not a sin, but the love of it is.

God favors neither the poor nor the wealthy. God blessed many of those He loved with wealth and considered them righteous. The question becomes, "Where do we go from here?" I believe we are *all* called to be our best for God. God calls us to rise up, in His name and by His strength. Therefore, if we have the opportunity, then we should push for more, so that we can bless others!

Question One
Did or do you believe that God favors the poor? If so, why? If not, why?

Question Two

Take a moment to close your eyes and think about your financial state. As you were reflecting, did you feel fearful when thinking about your finances? If so, what are some of the fears that you felt?

Question Three

In the video, we touched on supernatural provision. Have you ever had a time when you cried out to God and He supernaturally provided for you? If so, describe the situation below:

In some way, did your story require money or resources to come from somewhere or someone?

Question Four

In most instances, God does provide supernaturally for His children, but the money has to come from somewhere. When thinking about this, can you see the benefit of working out of poverty, if you have the opportunity, so that you might bless others who don't? Or helping to advance the missions of ministries for the Kingdom?

Question Five

Advancing forward is moving closer to and in our God-given mission. It is seizing the opportunity before us to become the best versions of us that we can be and, in turn, glorifying God. While this concept covers many areas in your life, reflect on your finances. Are you advancing forward or remaining stagnant? Describe how.

Question Six

In Matthew 19:16–22, Jesus reveals to the rich young ruler that he still lacked the ability to part with his stuff. His heart desired a closer relationship with God, but his wealth clouded his desire. This is the danger in wealth—we must continually stay focused on our Father in the midst of it so that we don't become attached and value it more than our relationship with God. Take a moment to reflect on all of your *stuff*. If you had to give up certain things in order to have eternal life, would you? Explain your reasoning.

Question Seven

The parable of the rich fool describes a man who saved his abundance until it was overflowing. He didn't have the *need* for everything he had, but somehow it must have fulfilled a void in his soul. It provided comfort for him that exceeded his desire to be closer to God.

When we looked at the story of Joseph, we saw that saving an abundance can be a good thing. It can not only provide for you in the future, but also for those who are in need. Do you feel like it's a sin to save money? If so, why? If not, why?

Exercise

Many of you going through this study are not *poor* by the world's standards. It can be tempting at times to feel poor when we are struggling financially, but I am confident that if you want to change your circumstances you can. Too often, I feel that some believers may use their financial struggles as a crutch because they feel that if they weren't struggling financially, they would be outside God's will. I struggle to believe that God has called us to live in financial turmoil. While not all of us aspire to cultivate wealth in our lifetimes, it does not glorify God to be continually struggling. It is our responsibility to manage our resources in a way that glorifies God. Just as we're called to understand what it means to live a life of righteousness, we're also called to live a life of generosity. The less we have, the harder it is to be generous (human nature).

Take a moment and ask yourself the following questions, and then determine what you can do to move toward generosity in your own life.

I fear having money because: **OR** I desire more money because:

I believe that God feels my feelings about money are:

Now, take a moment to reflect on what we've learned so far (or with the help of a Bible study tool) and back your answers up with Scripture. Be sure you take into account the full context of the verses you use.

Lesson 4—Video Guide

Handling Wealth Generously

Cultivating Abundance

- Abundance not only _____ for our family but if handled correctly can also _____ the _____ of God.

- If provided the opportunity, we all can cultivate an _____, but when we do, we are called to manage it _____.

- Wealth and possessions are a _____ from God.

- Ecclesiastes 5:19

  "Moreover, when God gives any man _____ and _____, and _____ him to enjoy them, to accept his lot and be happy in his work—this is a _____ from God."

- The word *gift* in Ecclesiastes 5:19 translates back to the Hebrew word *mattat,* which is defined as, "_____ _____."[1]

- It is not morally wrong to pursue abundance, but we must remain focused on _____ and not our stuff.

- Money possesses no _____ bias; it is simply a medium of _____. The _____ structure of money never changes; it is only in the hands of the _____, that money can assume a _____ slant.

• Heart matters are questions we have about specific things in our lives relating to how we're handling our abundance. Only _____ can enable you to consider these decisions correctly.

King Solomon

• When God asked King Solomon to ask anything of Him, King Solomon asked for only one thing: _____. (1 Kings 3:9)

• God not only blessed King Solomon with what he asked for, but also with _____ and _____. (1 Kings 3:11–14)

• While King Solomon was faithful for a while with the _____ and _____, his heart started to _____ away when he lost focus on being _____ to God.

• It was not King Solomon's wealth that was his _____, but his _____ in the midst of God's _____.

• The _____ of King Solomon became _____. (1 Kings 3–11)

Abraham

• Abraham was also a man of great _____, but unlike King Solomon, a man of lasting _____.

• Abraham was very wealthy in his life, with an abundance of _____, _____, and _____. (Gen. 13:2)

- Abraham acted out in _____ (Genesis 12:10–20) and _____ (Genesis 16:1–4), yet due to his persistent _____, he was _____ and so were the _____ after him.

Handling Abundance Generously

- Abundance does not always equate to _____ or _____ _____.

- It is out of our abundance that the Lord calls us to _____.

- 1 John 3:17

  "If anyone has _____ _____ and sees his brother in _____ but has no _____ on him, how can the _____ of God be in him?"

- _____ is not always a product of our _____.

- Generosity is a _____ of our _____.

- Generosity is the product of _____ and _____ coming together.

- In order to achieve generosity in our lives, we must first learn how to exercise _____ and _____.

Lesson 4—Personal Study

Handling Wealth Generously

Wealth often gets a bad rap in the Christian community. Why is that? This is especially boggling when a majority of ministries rely on large donations to survive. While wealth can corrupt good character—like we saw in King Solomon—when handled correctly it can be used to advance missions in many wonderful ways. Sometimes I wonder if we avoid wealth because we don't feel worthy of it?

For whatever reasons we may fear wealth, it is important to see it the way God does. Wealth is a blessing that can propel the mission of the Kingdom forward for ministries worldwide. It can lift children out of poverty and sex trafficking. It can spread the message of truth through evangelists, saving millions. It can distribute Bibles to the edges of the earth and much more.

Most of us are considered wealthy by the world's standards. Once we can see how, we can bless others out of our abundance and experience the supernatural joy; most of us won't want to stop. Through generosity we glorify God. Before we can be generous, we must learn not to fear wealth.

While becoming wealthy may not be everyone's goal, it is still important to recognize that those who posses wealth and manage it in a generous way should not be looked down upon (just like the poor). God has no favorites.

Question One
Read 2 Corinthians 9:6–15 about generosity. Reflect on what you read; and write down two things that stood out to you.

Question Two

Most people desire to achieve financial comfort. They desire to get out of the monthly cycle of struggling financially. Do you feel this way? Do you ever feel wrong for having these emotions? Do you believe God would want you to struggle?

Question Three

Ecclesiastes 5:19 states, "When God gives any man wealth and possessions, and enables him to enjoy them...this is a gift from God." Take a moment to list out ten gifts (possessions) from God that you have. Some examples might be your house, car, computer, and so forth.

Do you feel that it is wrong for you to own these things? If not, when do you think we can run into the trap of mismanaging what we have and dishonoring God?

Question Four

We've discussed that "money has no moral bias" and it is only in the "hands of the beholder that money can assume a moral slant." Do you feel that money possesses a moral bias? Why or why not?

Question Five

Heart matters are questions we have about how we're handling our finances where the Bible is not clear. Some examples might be the sizes of our houses or the types of cars we drive. For these things, we must consult with God in prayer to ensure that we are not entangling ourselves in idolatry. Take a moment to list out three heart matters with which you are wrestling. After you write them down, seek the Lord in prayer about these matters. A Christian is not a heathen if they live in a million-dollar house or a ten-million dollar house; sin enters their heart when they worship the house more than God.

Question Six

King Solomon was a man after God's heart (in the beginning), but soon he was corrupted by the poor choices he made in the midst of his wealth and honor. Solomon asked God for only one thing—a wise and discerning heart. If God came to you in this moment and told you that you could have anything that you wanted, what would you ask for (one thing)?

Question Seven

When we look at the story of Abraham versus King Solomon, we can see that continued obedience is the clear differentiator between the two. Do you feel that obedience correlates with God's blessings? Why or why not?

Question Eight

In examining generous giving, we reflected on the fact that generosity does not depend on abundance. This is clearly shown in the story of the poor widow. Though she gave less than anyone else, Jesus proclaimed that she gave more!

Have you ever been led by the Spirit to give out of your *lack*? If so, how did it turn out?

Exercise

Read 1 Kings 3–11. As you're reading, examine where Solomon's heart started and where it ended. Watch his heart shift. Take note of his attitudes and motivations and how those influenced how he conducted himself.

Take your notes below. Then when you're done, circle the point in your notes when his heart changed (or in your opinion, where he turned away from God).

What areas of your life can you monitor to ensure that you're protecting against financial idolatry?

What Is Tithing Today

The Old versus New Covenant

- We are under the _____ Covenant; therefore, we are _____ in Christ. We are no longer subject to be burdened by a _____ of _____.

- In Acts 15:10–11, Peter describes the Law as a _____ that was _____ for not only him, but also for the generations before him.

- Romans 8:1–4

  "Therefore, there is now _____ condemnation for those who are in Christ Jesus, because through Christ Jesus the law of the Spirit of life set me _____ from the law of sin and death. For what the law was _____ to do in that it was weakened by the sinful nature, God did by sending his own Son in the likeness of sinful man to be a sin offering. And so he condemned sin in sinful man, in order that the righteous requirements of the law might be fully _____ in us, who do not live according to sinful nature, but according to the Spirit."

- Romans 6:14

  "For sin shall not be your _____, because you are not under the _____, but under _____."

- Before _____ came, we were held _____ by the _____. (Galatians 3:23)

- Under the _____ Covenant, we have moved from a robotic way of _____ to one that _____ _____ God.

- A command under the _____ Covenant was _____ _____. Because we are under the _____ Covenant, we are no longer subject to this law.

Tithing Today

- Tithing 10 percent was a commandment from God, through Moses to the _____. It was a command under the _____ _____, which we are _____ longer subject to under the _____ Covenant.

- Replace the word *tithe* with the word _____. God wants _____ to be _____ and _____.

- When we're _____ about the _____ of who we're giving to, we give _____.

- 2 Corinthians 9:7
  "Each man should _____ what he has decided in his _____ to give, not _____ or under _____."

Generosity Today

- Generosity is not a product of _____ well-being, but a stance of the _____. It is not a _____ percentage of one's _____, but a desire to give toward something one believes in and supports.

- Generosity is an _____ of _____ toward God.

- In 2 Corinthians 8:1–5, the Macedonian churches gave out of what they had, even _____ what they had, in order to "_____ _____ _____" of Paul's mission! Not only did they desire to give, they _____.

- The motive for giving today should not be fueled by the _____, but by _____ and the _____ of God. There is much more freedom in this, opening up vast opportunity in the Kingdom.

2 Corinthians 9:6–15—Sowing Generously

- Verse 6

  What we put into something is what we will get _____ of it.

- Verse 7

  Giving should not be fueled by what we expect to get back from God, but by a pure _____ to give from our _____.

- Verse 8

  By God's _____ we will have what we need at _____ times so that we might be able to give according to His will.

- Verses 9–12

  The most beautiful picture of giving _____ is the fact that we in turn direct others to God. It is in our giving to them that they see the face of the _____.

- Verses 13–15

  Generosity becomes an expression of our _____ to others. It can serve as

  one of the key ingredients to helping change the hearts of people toward

  _____.

- Giving today goes beyond _____. We are not fulfilling a law in order to

  remain in _____ standing with God. Today we give generously because we

  desire to see the _____ of others met, and by our actions, direct them

  to _____.

Lesson 5—Personal Study

What Is Tithing Today

Tithing is a large topic in the church today. In most churches, only a small percentage of the members give regularly. Giving to the church is critical in supporting its mission. In order for any ministry to survive, it must have donors. So why is it that so many of us don't give to our churches? Is it a lack of funds or a lack of belief in the concept of tithing? Is it a distrust of how the funds will be used? The list goes on and on, but the Scriptures are clear. Under the New Covenant, we are called to be generous givers.

A generous giver gives in a cheerful manner, not reluctantly or under compulsion. A majority of the time, those who are giving to the church are giving because they think they have to. Perhaps they're giving under compulsion in an effort to remain in a good standing with God or the church's leadership.

Whatever may be fueling the giving in your church, it's important to understand what the Word of God has to say about this critical topic. I believe that when we can see how God is calling us to give today, our eyes will be opened to the joy of giving, that our giving can be further fueled by the Spirit, and we can partner with others to advance the Kingdom!

Question One
In the video, we discussed the Old versus New Covenant. We now reside under the New Covenant in Christ and are no longer burdened by the yoke of slavery. Was this a new way of thinking for you? Why or why not?

Question Two

Open your Bible to Romans 8:1–4, and write it below. What has Jesus Christ fulfilled in relation to the Law?

Question Three

When you read and wrote down Romans 8:1–4, what were some specific words or phrases that stood out to you? Do these verses inspire you to be free under God's grace?

Question Four

Tithing can be a sensitive subject for many believers because they have been taught their whole lives that giving 10 percent is what they are to do. Now that you see this commandment was given to the Israelites under the Mosaic Law, do you still feel pressure to tithe 10 percent? Why or why not?

Question Five

While we're no longer subject to the law of tithing 10 percent, giving today is critical. It is important that we financially support the ministries we believe in. Take a moment and think about your church. What is its mission?

Question Six

Regarding your church's mission, do you support and believe in it? If so, how does this correlate to your giving to your church? If not, how does this correlate to your giving to your church?

Question Seven

We are called to financially support not only the mission of our church but also other ministries that we're passionate about and the Spirit calls us to. Are there any other ministries that you can think of whose missions you are passionate about and would like to support?

Question Eight

Generous giving is a commission under the New Covenant. From what you've learned about generous giving, in what ways do you feel like you're giving generously? If you can't identify any current areas in which you are exhibiting generosity, then think of some areas in which you can and jot them down below.

Exercise

Some of the best verses on generous giving (today's tithe) can be found in 2 Corinthians 9:6–15. Open your Bible to these verses. Below, write down your thoughts on what is being said in each:

Verse 6

Verse 7

Verse 8

Verses 9–12

Verses 13–15

Part II: Live

Goal Setting and Budgeting

Freedom

- Most of us feel like budgets will equate to _____, but they actually bring _____ through _____.

- We must no longer allow _____ and _____ to hold us back from achieving a _____ financial well-being.

- Financial _____ and _____ are the beginning of freedom.

Goals

- Becoming financially free takes _____ and _____.

- When setting goals, it is important to be in tune with _____ _____ above all things. (James 4:13–16)

Budget

- Your _____ is a _____ tool that will help you accomplish your financial goals.

- Don't fret in making your budgeting experience _____; it takes time.

- Budgets are made up of four amounts relating to your income and expenses:

    1.

    2.

    3.

    4.

- In your budget, *money in* will always be _____, and *money out* will always be _____.

- A budget is worthless if you don't _____ your _____.

Create Your Budget

- Step One is to identify all sources of your _____ _____ _____.

- For households with a fluctuating income, set yourself a monthly _____.

- Step Two is to account for all of your _____ _____.

- Step Three is to calculate your _____ _____ _____.

Create a Positive Cash Flow

- If your cash flow is _____ each month, you need to examine your monthly _____ to determine how you can create a positive _____ _____.

- Instead of zeroing out your budget, create a _____.

Setting Goals and Budgeting

Why do budgets get a nasty name in the realm of personal finance? I hear that they take too much time and are pointless. Budgets can create the framework for where we're going financially. They can be critical to our success toward financial freedom. Even if we're in a position where our income is far exceeding our expenses, I still think that having a budget is critical to every household, just as it's a critical tool used in most businesses. But before we can create a budget, we have to first determine our goals.

Our financial goals will set the tone for how we set up our budget and where we tell the money to go. Without goals we are floating through life. The importance of setting goals in congruence with the Father's will is critical. So as you walk through the process of setting your goals, be sure to be in constant prayer and reflection to ensure that you are not wandering off the path.

Over the years, clients that I have seen who wholeheartedly implement a budget have been astoundingly successful! Whether it was in weathering financial storms or creating the income they needed to propel them forward, their focus and dedication paid off. It is my prayer that the same happens for you, but before this can happen, there must be a shift in your heart about this process. A budget is not pointless. It is not only for broke people. It is a strategic way of putting a plan in place so that you can assume the accountability over the money you manage.

Question One

Read the quote below and reflect on what true freedom in Christ looks like on the next page:

> "True freedom is, then, the exact opposite of what many people think. It is not freedom from all responsibility to God and to others, in order to live for my self. That is bondage to my own self-centeredness. Instead, true freedom is freedom from my silly little self, in order to live responsibly in love for God and others." (John R. W. Stott)[1]

Question Two

When most people think of budgets, they think restriction. They feel that the budget will rob them of the life they have been enjoying. When you think of a budget, what words come to mind?

Question Three

Fear and shame tend to be the key inhibitors to individuals facing their financial condition. As we know, these are not from God but from the enemy. In what ways do you feel like the enemy might be holding you back from facing your finances? What are the things that you are fearful or shameful of?

Question Four

Can you see how these lies from the enemy might be holding you back from experiencing the financial freedom that your spirit longs for? Take the enemy's words and replace them with truth below:

Question Five

The first step to goal setting and budgeting is *awareness*. Let's start with some basic questions; see if you can answer them. Don't worry about exact numbers—just write down what you think the answers might be:

    1. What was your net income last month?

    2. What were your total expenses?

    3. What was your cash flow?

*Note: when I ask these questions to groups of people, I find that they fall into one of three categories. The first group doesn't know the numbers and hasn't written them down. The second group kind of knows the numbers but doesn't have them written down. The third group concretely knows the numbers and has them written down. I encourage you to get to the place where you can just spit out these numbers as they relate to your finances.

Exercises

Exercise One—Establish Your Financial Goals

We first start with your financial goals. You will be writing down your top three financial goals for the next year. If you're married, your spouse will do the same. Then you will come together and determine three combined goals. In an effort to illustrate this, see the example below:

Example:

Individual Goals	Spouse's Goals	Combined Goals
1. Give more	1. Golf clubs	1. Give more
2. New bedding	2. Tool box	2. Pay off student loan
3. Gym membership	3. Give More	3. New carpet

You will notice that the individual goals are *specific* to the individual—as they should be. Since I started this process, I have always built enjoyment into it for clients. There is nothing rewarding about working your tail off, only to not enjoy some of the fruits of your labor.

Here is the deal, though—if you are married, your first goal is to knock off one of your combined goals, and then try to meet one individual goal each. This is over the course of one year, so there should be plenty of time. These goals also need to be weighed against where the Spirit leads you to give and your necessities (expenses, savings, debt, etc.). These extras give you something to work for and toward verses feeling like you're a slave to yourself.

Now it's your turn. If you're single, you will only fill out the first column below.

Individual Goals	Spouse's Goals	Combined Goals

Exercise Two—Create Your Budget

Now that you have your goals established, it's time to create your budget! We are going to take this step by step. Complete the activity for each step. This process will be explained manually for those without access to Microsoft Excel. If you do have access to Microsoft Excel, I strongly encourage you to download the MAP Budget Tool. This is a budget in electronic form via an Microsoft Excel spreadsheet and it will automate much of the budgeting process for you. You can download the MAP Budget Tool at www. TheStewardshipMovement.com. If you don't use Microsoft Excel, each of these steps are detailed enough for you to follow along in a ruled notebook. Let's go!

Step One

The first step is to identify all the sources of your net monthly income. Your net income is the income that you *take* home after taxes and other deductions.

Think of it as pulling up fish onto a boat with a net. The fish that you pull up and onto your boat (with the net) is your *net*—what you'll bring home. The *gross* represents the total number of fish in your net before you brought it up (some of the fish are lost through the net in the process of pulling it up to the boat).

Your gross income is reduced to your net because of things taken out, like health insurance, taxes, social security, retirement-account contributions, and so forth. While some recommend utilizing gross income when creating a budget, I've found it easiest for clients to utilize net. Again, the goal is to not turn you into an analytical math whiz, but to broaden your understanding of where your money is going. If you're doing this process manually, I recommend that you start your budget in a blank, ruled notebook. On the first page, you are going to write down the first draft of your budget. For illustration purposes we will be referring to Tom and Sarah's budget as we did in the video.

First, at the top of the page, make a header that says *Budget*. Then, write down your net monthly income in the format shown on the next page and total it up. Be sure to leave space for two additional columns to the left and to the right of your *Budgeted* column that we'll be adding later.

BUDGET

Income	Budgeted
Tom Paycheck #1	$1750
Tom Paycheck #2	$1750
Total Income	**$3500**

Step Two

Next, below your income, write down your expenses in the format shown and then total them up.

BUDGET

Income	Budgeted
Tom Paycheck #1	$1750
Tom Paycheck #2	$1750
Total Income	**$3500**

Expenses	Budgeted
Giving	($350)
Mortgage—Primary	($1125)
Utilities—Electrical, Water	($175)
Internet and Home Phone	($87)
Cell Phones	($81)
Insurance—Auto	($99.25)
Insurance—Life	($22.50)
Spending Money	($100)
Entertainment	($100)
Groceries	($600)
Gasoline	($200)
Savings	($50)
Credit Card	($20)
Student Loan	($79)
Car Loan #1	($225)
Car Loan #2	($180)
Personal Care	($60)

Miscellaneous	($25)
Total Expenses	**($3578.75)**

Following are a few important notes about the *expenses.*

First, notice the parentheses around the amounts. While I don't expect you all to be math whizzes, I do want you to understand the basic *flow* of money. Money *in* is **positive.** Money *out* is **negative.** The parentheses indicate money going out. Whenever you are inputting or writing down expenses, get in the habit of putting the number in parentheses.

Second, notice how I didn't just round everything. When writing down your expenses, don't just guess or round the totals. Go to your statements and write down the exact amounts. For expenses like groceries and gas, your budgeted number will be rounded because these items don't have a bill amount associated with them.

Third, this is a very basic expense list that does not include all of the expense categories I have seen over the years, so don't stop here. This is just an example, so be sure to evaluate all of your expenses for the month and just use this as a guide.

Step Three

Calculate your monthly cash flow. Your monthly cash flow is calculated by subtracting your expenses from your income. For this example, the calculation would look like this:

Monthly Income	-	Monthly Expenses	=	Monthly Cash Flow
$3500		($3578.75)		($78.75)

As you can see, Tom and Lisa are driving a negative monthly cash flow. When people first construct their budget, a lot of them see a negative cash flow. We will address how to correct this later. For now, I just want you to get these numbers down.

Step Four

Flip to a new piece of a paper in your notebook, a few pages after your budget. At the top of this page, make a header that says *Budget Tracking.*

This sheet is to simply track your expenses on a weekly basis; after all, what is the point of a budget if you're not tracking your expenses each week to ensure that you are not going over budget?

On this sheet, you'll list the date that you spent money, where you spent money, how much money you spent, and what category on your budget this amount should be assigned to. Record this information in the format shown below.

BUDGET TRACKING

8/1	Tom Paycheck #1	$1750	Income
8/9	Vitamin Store	($89.19)	Groceries
8/9	Grocery Store	($125.14)	Groceries
8/15	Café	($28.19)	Entertainment
8/17	Cleaners	($12.58)	Miscellaneous

On a weekly basis, you will tabulate these totals and ensure that you are not going over your budgeted amounts. You will have some expenses that will always be the same, such as your mortgage or insurance. For expenses like gas, groceries, and entertainment, you will have to measure them against your budget. For instance, the grocery budget for Tom and Lisa is $600 per month. So far, they have spent $214.33 as depicted in the tracking above. This means that they have $385.67 left for groceries.

Step Five

Now that you have your budget created on the first page and your tracking sheet started, it is time to flip back to your Budget sheet. We are going to add one column to the left and one to the right of your *Budgeted* column.

On your Budget sheet, add a column to the left of the *Budgeted* column with the heading *Actual*. Then, to the right of the *Budgeted* column, add a column with the heading *Remainder*. Then, log any actual expenses for the month so far under the *Actual* column from your Tracking Sheet.

You will be updating these columns on a weekly basis according to your Tracking Sheet, so you will need to use pencil for these. Each week, under the *Actual* column, you are going to record when income and expenses are realized. For expenses that accrue over the month like gas and groceries, you will need to add these and update the amounts. The *Remainder* column is then the difference between what you budgeted for and what you have actually spent.

Create these columns in the format as shown on the next page.

BUDGET

Income	Actual	Budgeted	Remainder
Tom Paycheck #1	$1750	$1750	$0
Tom Paycheck #2	$0	$1750	$1750
Total Income	**$1750**	**$3500**	**$1750**

Expenses	Actual	Budgeted	Remainder
Giving	($0)	($350)	$350
Mortgage—Primary	($0)	($1125)	$1125
Utilities—Electrical, Water	($0)	($175)	$175
Internet and Home Phone	($0)	($87)	$87
Cell Phones	($0)	($81)	$81
Insurance—Auto	($0)	($99.25)	$99.25
Insurance—Life	($0)	($22.50)	$22.50
Spending Money	($0)	($100)	$100
Entertainment	($28.19)	($100)	$71.81
Groceries	($214.33)	($600)	$385.67
Gasoline	($0)	($200)	$200
Savings	($0)	($50)	$50
Credit Card	($0)	($20)	$20
Student Loan	($0)	($79)	$79
Car Loan #1	($0)	($225)	$225
Car Loan #2	($0)	($180)	$180
Personal Care	($0)	($60)	$60
Miscellaneous	($12.58)	($25)	$12.42
Total Expenses	**($255.10)**	**($3578.75)**	**$3323.65**

This is how you can budget manually; I don't want anyone to miss the opportunity to learn how to budget if they don't have access to Microsoft Excel. Yet, in an effort to save you time, I would strongly urge you to work toward getting the MAP Budget Tool. It will save you time—budget for it! You can get the MAP Budget Tool at www. TheStewardshipMovement.com.

Create a Positive Cash Flow

Now that we have created the skeleton for Tom and Lisa's budget, it is time that we address their cash-flow issue—a negative cash flow. Just like them, when you run your budget, you may find that your monthly net income minus expenses is a negative number. If this is the case, know that you're not alone. When I first met with clients, many would find themselves from a ($100) to ($500) cash flow monthly. They could not understand how this was happening because they were not feeling the pinch. But you can't spend negative money. Either savings or credit cards were supplementing the difference. We will talk about how to correct this soon, but before we do, let's keep moving down the path for creating a positive cash flow together (this includes those of you who are not driving a negative cash flow each month).

Some financial counselors will counsel that you *zero* out your budget (which is not a bad plan), but I am going to suggest you do something differently to create a padding for yourself, a cushion. A cushion is a safety net that you build up for yourself. Think of it like overdraft protection. It is money left over after expenses. You don't spend it, but it gives you the comfort of knowing that you have more than zero in the end, as one of my clients called it, "The new zero!" Yes, indeed, it is your new zero! Your cushion amount is up to you. It depends on how much you have left over and what feels comfortable. Typical cushion amounts are $100, $250, $300, or $500. This means that instead of your income minus expenses equaling zero, they will equal your cushion. Be sure to continue any overdraft protection that you have on your accounts—this is just a good measure.

In regard to Tom and Lisa's budget (and yours, too, if you are driving a negative cash flow each month), in order to create a positive cash flow, we will need to first cut expenses. As we're cutting expenses we will also work to create a positive cushion for them. A cushion is an amount that will be built up over time according to your budget. Once you reach your goal cushion amount and it's in your bank account, you can then zero out your budget if you would like.

As you're looking through Tom and Lisa's budget, be reflecting on your own budget. Highlight the items that may be considered *nonessentials*. These might include items like entertainment or spending money. You may not have to eliminate these entirely, just reduce the amount you allocate towards them each month.

On Tom and Lisa's budget, I have starred the items that needed to be reduced in order to create a positive cash flow.

Tom and Lisa's Revised Budget

BUDGET

Income	Actual	Budgeted	Remainder
Tom Paycheck #1	$1750	$1750	$0
Tom Paycheck #2	$0	$1750	$1750
Total Income	**$1750**	**$3500**	**$1750**

Expenses	Actual	Budgeted	Remainder
Giving	($0)	($350)	$350
Mortgage—Primary	($0)	($1125)	$1125
Utilities—Electrical, Water	($0)	($175)	$175
Internet and Home Phone	($0)	($87)	$87
Cell Phones	($0)	($81)	$81
Insurance—Auto	($0)	($99.25)	$99.25
Insurance—Life	($0)	($22.50)	$22.50
*Spending Money	**($0)**	**($0)**	**$0**
*Entertainment	**($28.19)**	**($50)**	**$21.81**
Groceries	($214.33)	($600)	$385.67
Gasoline	($0)	($200)	$200
Savings	($0)	($50)	$50
Credit Card	($0)	($20)	$20
Student Loan	($0)	($79)	$79
Car Loan #1	($0)	($225)	$225
Car Loan #2	($0)	($180)	$180
Personal Care	($0)	($60)	$60
Miscellaneous	($12.58)	($25)	$12.42
Total Expenses	**($255.10)**	**($3428.75)**	**$3173.65**

Tom and Lisa's Revised Cash Flow

Monthly Income	-	Monthly Expenses	=	Monthly Cash Flow
$3500		($3428.75)		$71.25

While we have achieved a positive cash flow for Tom and Lisa, they are not paying down their debt any faster. Saving and paying down debt is dependent on one thing—income. If your income only covers your essential expenses and minimum payments on your credit cards and loans, the rate of your debt-reduction and savings will be much slower.

Now it's your turn. Take a moment to reflect on your budget. What expenses might you be able to reduce or eliminate in order to create a positive cash flow each month? Make these changes to your budget either in your notebook or in the MAP Budget Tool now. Keep working the numbers until you get a positive number.

As I stated earlier, if you try and try, and just can't get that bottom line to be positive, or if you make it positive by setting unrealistic expectations for yourself, then the only solution might be increasing your income.

Tracking Spending

The last item that we're going to talk about in this lesson is tracking your spending. If you want to meet your financial goals, then you will need to track your spending. In the earlier steps when setting up your budget, you set up your Tracking Sheet, now here's a further explanation of how to use it.

Say your gas budget is $200 per month. Every time you fill up, deduct what you spent from the budgeted amount so you know what you have left to spend for the month. This is your weekly accountability process.

Continue to use your Budget and Tracking Sheet in conjunction with each other. If you are married, you and your spouse need to be on the same page as far as your budget. One of you needs to be the Tracker. If you are single, then you're it. The Tracker is responsible for logging all spending against the budget to ensure you're staying on track. That means every week, you need to update your *Actual* and *Remainder* columns to ensure you are not overspending. If you're married, it's also the Tracker's responsibility to get a copy of the budget to the other spouse. That way your spouse always has an up-to-date understanding of where the budget stands.

Note: the Tracker is *not* the permission giver, nor the source of all budget information. It is still the Nontracker's responsibility to be in touch with the budget every week. Everyone is responsible for the spending. Stay away from the blame game.

For those of you doing the budget by hand, be sure to keep the budget notebook in a place that either of you can go to reference it at any time. For those using the MAP Budget Tool, I recommend utilizing a file sharing service that both you and your spouse can access remotely. My husband and I do this, and it keeps both of us on the same page at all times. By sharing a copy of the budget, you have it to reference if you are apart and you're trying to make wise financial choices.

Tackling Debt

About Debt

- Most of us have to utilize _____ for _____ _____.

- Instead of making _____ _____ the goal, why don't we first make

  handling it _____ _____ the goal?

- When we're in debt, we are _____, _____, _____,

  and _____.

- When we _____ other people _____, we can't feel _____.

- Proverbs 22:7

  "The _____ rule over the _____, and the _____ is _____

  to the _____."

- Three important biblical principles regarding debt:

  1. Pay back _____ debt that you borrow.   Psalm _____ : _____

  2. Pay back your debts _____.   Prov. _____ : ____-____

  3. Stay _____ of debt when you can.   Prov. _____ : _____

Pressing Forward

- The story of the Widow's Oil in 2 Kings 4:1–7 is an amazing depiction of what we're called to do when we're in debt:

  Take _____

  Ask for _____

  Take _____

- With concentrated _____ and _____, most of us can pay off our debt.

- Your _____ will be your key tool to achieving your debt-reduction goals.

Debt-Reduction Strategies

- Strategy #1—High Interest:

  This strategy prioritizes paying the _____ interest debts _____.

- Strategy #2—Low Balance:

  This strategy prioritizes paying the _____ balance debts _____.

- Whichever strategy you use, utilize the _____ method for each.

Your Mortgage

- Are you ready to pay off your mortgage? Three questions to ask yourself:

  1.

  2.

  3.

Tackling Debt

Your budget is a tool to help you accomplish your goals, but it doesn't stop there. Not only do you have to utilize your budget on a weekly basis, but also you have to implement a strategy to knock out your debt and pump up your savings. This lesson will help you to strategize how to pay down your debt. It will also give you direction on what debt to pay first and how much. There is nothing more exciting than seeing the finish line in regard to your debt and, even better, crossing that finish line.

The most important thing I want you to remember in this process is that any debt feels like a lot. I have worked with clients who have $20,000 in debt and others with $150,000 (not including their mortgage). Debt of any size feels like a lot—because it is. It's bondage. Let's learn how to tackle it and eliminate it one day at a time.

Question One

When you think of debt, write down five words that come to mind:

Question Two

From what we've discussed so far, can you see how debt can keep people in bondage? What are some of the things that debt prevents you from doing?

Question Three

In the video we discussed three biblical principles regarding debt:

1. Pay back all debt that you borrow.
2. Pay back your debts promptly.
3. Stay out of debt, when you can.

If you started applying these principles to how you managed your debt today, what do you think would be different about your financial picture one year from now?

Question Four

Take a moment to read the story of the Widow's Oil in 2 Kings 4:1–7. What are some lessons you're able to extract from this story in regard to how you can better address your current debts?

Question Five

We discussed two debt-reduction strategies—high interest and lowest balance. Which strategy will you use to pay down your debt and why?

Exercise

Now for the fun part—we get to see all the numbers on one page and strategically plan how we're going to eliminate the debt! Again, we will approach this using the two methods above. If you would prefer a more automated approach, you can utilize the debt-reduction tool found on www.TheStewardshipMovement.com.

In this section you will find the manual instructions for creating a debt-reduction plan; they can also be used in conjunction with setting up your plan in the debt-reduction tool as well.

Step One—Write Down Your Debt

In order to do this step, you need to have detailed information on all of your debts: the company that you owe, the interest rate you are paying, your most recent balance, and your minimum payment amount.

Do not take this step lightly. Make sure all the information is accurate and complete so you can have a real picture of your debt.

Flip to a new page in your notebook. On the top of the page, write the header *Debt-Reduction Plan*. Then, write down the information for your debts in the format shown below. For this example, we will review Tom and Lisa's debt.

DEBT-REDUCTION PLAN

Creditor	Balance	Interest Rate	Min. Payment
Car Loan #1	$4000	7%	$225
Credit Card	$541.24	8.95%	$20
Student Loan	$7857.64	5%	$79
Car Loan #2	$7652.49	6%	$180

Step Two—Solidify Your Debt-Reduction Budget

Now determine your debt-reduction budget. In the example above, the total minimum debt payments add up to $504. Since the debt-reduction budget is $550, there is an additional $46 that can be allocated toward the debts.

Step Three—Select Your Strategy

A majority of the time, I would recommend the *low balance* strategy to clients. It is the most rewarding and exciting, and when we're talking about debt, we need this!

I would encourage you to look at your debt and the interest rates, and then think through which plan will help you reach your goals fastest. And, as always, pray for guidance and, if married, talk this over with your spouse.

Step Four—Prioritize Your Debts

Once you have settled on your strategy, reorganize the order of your debts in your notebook. In the example, I am going to recommend that Tom and Lisa utilize the low balance strategy. Therefore, we will reorganize their debts from priority one, down to priority four as shown. Then, add the extra amount to the first debt ($20+$46).

DEBT-REDUCTION PLAN

Creditor	Balance	Interest Rate	Min. Payment
Credit Card	$541.24	8.95%	$66
Car Loan #1	$4000	7%	$225
Car Loan #2	$7652.49	6%	$180
Student Loan	$7857.64	5%	$79

We have reorganized the order in which these debts appear because we want to knock out the lowest balance first; therefore, the credit card becomes the first debt we're going to eliminate.

Step Five—Update Your Budget

Once you have calculated how much you will be paying toward your debts each month, be sure to update your budget with these numbers. Tom and Lisa would need to update their budget to reflect $66 each month for the credit card versus $20. Keep track of your debt-reduction totals on this sheet as you move along.

Step Six—Celebrate

Remember to celebrate as you pay off debts! This is a *huge* accomplishment and takes dedication and focus.

Creating Savings

The Balance

- Saving money is just as important as _____ off _____.

- Even if all of your debt is _____ off and you have _____ savings, if a major expense hits, you'll be back in _____ because you have no _____.

- There can be a balance between both paying off _____ and _____.

Hoarding versus Provision

- When the Bible was written, wealth existed in the form of _____, _____, _____, _____, _____, _____, and _____. These commodities were either _____ or utilized to _____ others.

- Saving money for the future is _____ not _____.

- Wealth saved for the future can be used for _____ and to _____ others.

Short-Term Savings (STS)

- Short-Term Savings (STS) is an account where you set aside a portion of your _____ into each month to pay for expenses. All of these expenses will have to be paid for. Some examples include:

- The purpose of the STS account is to protect you against _____ expenses so that you have the cash you need when the bill comes due.

- It also acts as a place where you can build up _____ toward _____ items such as:

- Your STS account will build _____ into your finances.

Long-Term Savings (LTS)

- Long-Term Savings (LTS) is your _____ savings fund. It also needs to be in _____ form.

Future Savings

- Your future savings is an account that you set up with a licensed professional to ensure that you have sufficient income for future _____ and to _____ others.

Creating Savings

Too many times I hear stories of people paying off loads of debt, throwing a party, and stopping there. Paying off debt is critical to your financial success, but so is saving money. The most important thing to remember is that even if all of your debt is paid off, if you have a major expense come up with no savings, you'll end up back in debt. I want you to accomplish major milestones in slashing your debt, but I also want you to build up your savings at the same time.

Let's face it—we all have needs. These include food, clothing, water, and shelter. While we're living, we will always have these needs, and they require money. There will come a time in our lives when we may no longer be able to physically work, or we choose not to. When this time comes, our needs will still cost money. Therefore, savings is not only a critical component to extra padding in life but also the main source of income in our later years.

In Matthew 6:25–34, Jesus urges us not to worry about what we will eat, drink, or wear. I don't believe this is a commission from Jesus to think these things will appear out of thin air. This commission goes deeper and touches back on what we spoke about in the earlier lessons; we are called not to *focus* on these things. Have you ever met anyone stressed out about these things, stressed out about money? Do you think that in all that worry and stress they can be effective for God? Be obedient to Christ where you feel He has called you. Work hard and stay focused on Him.

Question One

When you think about savings, do you think it's a sinful act? Why or why not?

Question Two

Do you believe that God calls believers to save? If so, then for what?

Question Three

The Bible offers many examples of how individuals saved to hoard their wealth or how they saved to provide for themselves and others. Take a moment to read the verses below and reflect on whether you feel it's a depiction of hoarding or providing.

2 Chronicles 31:11–12

2 Kings 20:13

2 Chronicles 32:27–29

Deuteronomy 14:28–29

Nehemiah 10:37–38

Isaiah 10:28

Genesis 41:41–57

Question Four

A depiction of saving for provision is when God commands Noah to store food for himself and the animals in Genesis 6:21. Take a moment and read Genesis 6:9–22. Can you see the wisdom in storing away for future provision here? For further study, read Proverbs 6:6–8 and Proverbs 30:25. Describe how storing for the future can provide for even the smallest of creatures.

Question Five

It is considered wise not only to store up for future provision but also not to consume what you're storing up for the future. Write out the following verses:

Proverbs 21:17

Proverbs 21:20

Question Six

The more we get into this, the more we learn that savings isn't sinful; rather, what is sinful is hoarding wealth to boast about it or to build our identity upon it. Take a moment to reflect on your savings situation. Are you confident that your decisions up to this point are leading you in a wise direction? If not, what can you change, starting today?

Exercise

Now that we have addressed savings from a biblical perspective, we can venture into the practical.

Saving is a valuable tool that we can use to provide for current and future events. As you set up your savings plan, there will be two types: Long-Term Savings (LTS) and Short-Term Savings (STS).

Setting Up Your STS

Your STS account should be managed via a checking or savings account with a bank. It needs to be in the form of liquid funds and an account that you can transfer to and from without penalties or fees. I recommend you use a savings account. This account is the storeroom for funds set to be allocated to cover expenses involving automobile, household, personal care, clothing, pet care, gifts, travel, periodic bills, and more. This section gives you step-by-step instructions on how to get your own STS set up today. You will not believe the freedom that your STS will add to your life! You can use these instructions if you're manually tracking or using the MAP Budget Tool.

Step One—Determine the Account

Many people have multiple savings and checking accounts. If this is you, determine which account you can dedicate to your STS. If you don't have one, open a savings or checking account through your bank.

Step Two—Create Categories

Now, flip to a new page in your notebook, and at the top create the header *Short-Term Savings*. It's time to come up with your categories.

Determine your necessity categories first. For most, these include automobile, household, personal care, clothing, pet care, gifts, and periodic bills. These are all of the expenses that you will eventually *need* money for: you have to budget for them.

Once you have created your essential categories, you may have additional cash flow that you can contribute toward nonessential categories—categories like travel, home decorations, improvements, and so forth. If so, create a line between these two areas as shown in the following example:

Auto

Home

Personal Care

Clothing

Gifts

Trash Service (quarterly)

Life Insurance (annually)

Travel

Step Three—Determine STS Budget

In order to create your STS budget, add up your essentials and determine how much you need to set aside each month for each. For example, if your trash service is a quarterly bill, take the total, $69, and divide it by three. That means you need to set aside $23 each month for this bill. As for varying expenses—like auto, home, clothing, personal care—review your expenses for these categories over the last twelve months and average them out. So, let's pretend that when you do this, you have found that you spent $240 over the last twelve months on personal care. To determine how much you need to set aside each month, divide $240 by twelve. This equals $20 that you will need to set aside each month for this category. Now, update your STS sheet in the format as shown below to determine your STS budget. For the example, we will refer back to Tom and Lisa. You will notice that the *Amount* for some of the categories is $0. That is because Tom and Lisa don't have the income at this time to support putting money into these categories; they will require an increase in income.

SHORT-TERM SAVINGS

Category	Amount (12 mo.)	Monthly Budget
Auto	$0	$0
Home	$0	$0
Personal Care	$240	$20
Clothing	$240	$20
Gifts	$600	$50
Trash Service (quarterly)	$69	$23
Life Insurance (annually)	$270	$22.50
Travel	$0	$0

The STS budget for Tom and Lisa is $135.50 per month.

When individuals first determine their STS budget, they are a little taken back. They think, "I can't afford to allocate that much to savings!" It is important to remember that this is savings for future provision. You will need the money for these items in the near future; therefore, the money must be set aside. If you don't, how can you plan to pay for them in the future—hope that the money is there when the need arises? If the money is not there when the need arises you will be required to go into debt or utilize savings.

This has been one of the hardest practices I have had to implement with our own finances. Our STS budget is currently $622 per month. This is a discipline, and it might hurt a little bit. This is where a lot of us start to feel the pinch, but the STS holds us accountable, preventing us from spending frivolously and then freaking out when these expenses come up and the money isn't there. Now, I say all of this in regard to your essential categories. For the additional fun categories like travel, home decorations, improvements, and so forth, these are secondary. You may not have the extra income to allocate toward these at this time. Yet over time, as you free up more cash flow, you will be able to save toward these fun categories as well!

Step Four—Add to Budget

Now that you have a budget for your STS account, be sure to add a STS line item on your budget, with the specified amount.

Tom and Lisa will need to update their budget by eliminating their personal care and life insurance and lumping those into their STS category on their budget.

Step Five—Tracking Your STS Account

Since your STS account is one account and a pool of money, you need to track this pool of money according to each category so you know how much of this pool you can access for each category. If you are utilizing the MAP Budget Tool, then this gets tracked for you after putting in your categories and some other basic data. If you are tracking this manually, then you will follow a similar process to your budget tracking. Use a pencil, as the category balances will be constantly be changing.

On the next page there is an example of how to track your STS account. Below the listing of your categories, you will track your monthly expenses against your various categories. You will also need to add the columns as shown.

SHORT-TERM SAVINGS

Current Balance	Category	Money In	Money Out	Bal.
$0	Auto	$0	$0	$0
$0	Home	$0	$0	$0
$0	Personal Care	$20	($15.45)	$4.55
$0	Clothing	$20	$0	$20
$0	Gifts	$50	($25)	$25
$0	Trash Service (quarterly)	$23	$0	$23
$0	Life Insurance (annually)	$22.50	$0	$22.50
$0	Travel	$0	$0	$0

Tracking:

8/4	Beauty	($15.45)	Personal Care
8/15	Mart Inc.	($25.00)	Gifts

There you have it—your own STS account tracking sheet! You are now well on your way to greater freedom in this area. As I mentioned earlier, this system has helped Stephen and me tremendously. I have seen it transform the financial state of many clients, as well. I pray that it is a beneficial tool for you and your family, too. Now, let's move on to your LTS account.

Setting Up Your LTS

Just like your STS account, your LTS account should be managed via a savings account with a bank. It needs to be in the form of liquid funds and an account that you can transfer to and from without penalties or fees.

As noted earlier, this account is your emergency savings fund. This account consists of monies that you can access in the event of a job loss or major medical emergency. It should not be used for any of the STS categories that we have discussed so far. This account can easily be set up through your bank, or you can designate one of your current savings accounts to be your LTS. Here are five easy steps to get your LTS set up today:

Step One—Determine the Account

Determine which savings account you can dedicate to your LTS. If you don't have one, then open a savings account through your bank.

Step Two—Write Out Your Milestones

In your notebook, flip to a new page after your STS tracking sheet and at the top write the header *Long-Term Savings*. Write out your milestones in the format as shown below.

LONG-TERM SAVINGS

Milestone	Amount
Milestone #1	$1,000
Milestone #2	$3,000
Milestone #3	$5,000
Milestone #4	$10,000
Milestone #5	Six Months' Income
Milestone #6	Twelve Months' Income

Step Three—Determine LTS Budget

The amount you have to allocate to your LTS will be dependent upon several things. Here is a priority chart that you can utilize each month to help determine how much to put into your LTS:

Priority #1—Giving
Priority #2—Bills and STS (essential categories)
Priority #3—Debt-Reduction, LTS, and Future Savings (balance)
Priority #4—STS (nonessential categories)

Step Four—Add to Budget

By weighing these priorities and examining your budget, you should have an amount that you can allocate to your LTS. Don't be discouraged if you don't have much of anything or zero to allocate toward your LTS. This can be the hardest area to grow; that is why creating small milestones can be so helpful!

Step Five—Tracking Your LTS Account

It's important to track your progress against your LTS milestones each month. To start this process, you will need to set date goals for each milestone—the date on which you feel like you can hit that goal. So for example, if your LTS budget is $50 per month, it will take you twenty months to hit your first milestone.

Write that date down next to the milestone as shown if you are tracking manually. If you are using the MAP Budget Tool, you will be able to utilize the tab provided.

LONG-TERM SAVINGS

Milestone	Amount	Goal Date
Milestone #1	$1,000	MM/YYYY
Milestone #2	$3,000	
Milestone #3	$5,000	
Milestone #4	$10,000	
Milestone #5	Six Months' Income	
Milestone #6	Twelve Months' Income	

Awesome job—you now officially have created both your STS and LTS accounts to create the majority of your savings plan! Your next step is to sit down with a licensed professional and determine how much you can allocate in your budget toward future income. The goal is to get a plan in place so that you know that you will have sufficient income in the future.

As we discussed at the beginning of this chapter, savings is a very important piece of our financial wellness. We have also learned that when we save, we are not participating in an unbiblical or ungodly process. You now have not only the biblical foundation for God's view of money, but also the practical steps to get your financial house in order.

We now come to the last topic: translating all that you have learned into legacy. The conclusion is the finale of your training phase. You are now ready to stir up *The Stewardship Movement* within your family, church, and community!

Conclusion

The Stewardship Movement isn't about you. It's about your family, your church, and your community. It's about legacy.

Your legacy consists of what you do for those you shared life with—family, friends, church members, and even strangers. Your legacy is the series of footprints that your life leaves on the hearts of those you serve. It extends beyond how you're remembered. **Your legacy is eternal.**

Part of what makes up a legacy is the way we manage the resources that God entrusts us with today. The way we manage these resources not only affects our families and those we serve, but also the Kingdom.

My goal for you is that your legacy is one that reflects brightly with regard to your financial management and even further than this, one that eternally impacts the lives of all those around you.

The Stewardship Movement is about sharing what you've learned with others so that they, too, may live out a life of **eternal impact**—a life that creates movement in the lives around them, movement in the Kingdom, movement in advancing a common mission and goal, and movement that is not hindered by *financial chaos.*

Your legacy starts now by living out all you've learned, while also equipping others, to steward their resources the same way. Together, we can live out what we've learned about biblical financial stewardship and then share with others how to do the same.

If this study changed your perspective on money and finances and you desire to share this message with others you care about, lead a small group! Get all the tools you need to lead a small group today; visit the link below.

I am confident that united as the body of Christ, we can create a bigger, eternal legacy—one that glorifies the Father and advances the Kingdom!

**Start your own
Stewardship Movement
today at:**

www.TheStewardshipMovement.com

About the Author

Katelyn Swiatek is the founder of MAP Financial Solutions alongside her husband, Stephen. Katelyn is passionate about equipping Christians with the principles of biblical financial stewardship. Equipped with these truths, the body of Christ can live out their mission; bringing glory to God through generosity. She and her husband enjoy backpacking all over the world; including in their own backyard of Colorado.

If you would like Katelyn to come speak at your church, contact her at info@mapfinancialsolutions.com.

Notes

Lesson 2—Video Guide

1. Edward W. Goodrick and John R. Kohlenberger III, *The Strongest NIV Exhaustive Concordance* (Grand Rapids, MI: Zondervan, 1999), 892–893.

2. "Poverty," United Nations and CyberSchoolBus, *Briefing Papers*, accessed February 24, 2015, https://web.archive.org/web/20101116183705/http://www.un.org/Pubs/CyberSchoolBus/briefing/poverty/index.htm.

3. Randy Alcorn, *The Law of Rewards* (Carol Stream, IL: Tyndale, 2003), accessed December 15, 2014, http://www.epm.org/static/uploads/downloads/book-resources/Law_of_Rewards.pdf.

Lesson 4—Video Guide

1. Edward W. Goodrick and John R. Kohlenberger III, *The Strongest NIV Exhaustive Concordance* (Grand Rapids, MI: Zondervan, 1999), 1448.

Lesson 6—Personal Study

1. John R. W. Stott, *The Contemporary Christian: Applying God's Word to Today's World* (Downers Grove, IL: InterVarsity, 1992), 55.